HER HEART & SOUL

SAMAIRA

i would like to thank

the 12 year old me

for picking pen that day

and making all this possible .

Contents

Contents

Contents

Contents

Contents

Contents

Foreword

she knew who she
    was meant to be ,
    so kept fighting till it
    turned her way

Preface

This book is a form of simplicity of short and crisp poetry inspired by some moments of my life.

all these poems convey different emotions and different feelings and thus are on different subjects

i hope some will make you laugh , cry , angry and heartbroken at the same time .

they will give you the feeling of love , hate and will make you remember your firsts .

i had never thought of publishing these memories in the form of a poetry book ,

but here they lay infront of you all in its raw form.

enjoy the journey dear reader that has taken me four years to conquer .

Acknowledgements

i would like to thank my nanu
  for always showering his blessings
  on me.
  i love you and i miss you.

Prologue

this book is my heart & soul
   here in your hands
   make sure to keep it safe
   till the very end of the trip
   because my love
   i trust you the most

1. maa

the one who burns
her own
heart
to ignite yours
truly maa you are
my angel

2. writing

• 2 •

writing comes to me
in waves
and tonight i am
drowning

3. his voice

your voice melted me
like a snowman
at the start of early summer

4. milk & honey

• 4 •

you make me see myself
like milk and honey
being the prettiest girl
you had ever seen

5. closeness

we are so close
yet years apart

6. meaning of life

i learned the meaning of
life at quite a young age
with
school bag on my back
and tears in my eyes
when you left us
in search of a new place

7. silence in her eyes

she was a silent tsunami
an earthquake that
could shake the entire
earth

8. chocolate

she wanted to get draped in
chocolate,
hide all her wounds behind
its sweetness.
so that the world could only
taste her favourite part
and not what lies beneath that
cocoa draping
yet she was a little girl before
the world turned her into
a monster.

9. by choice

• 9 •

liking you was an
accident
loving you was
my choice

10. scars

all my scars bleed
and scream your name

11. you are loved

•11•

who made you
feel like you are
not worth the efforts
my dear

12. to cheat

my therapist asked
young girl
who broke your heart
i replied
i broke his

13. mother

if somebody asked
me whom i admire
the most
is always going
to be you maa

14. mistakes

chill babe
we are just humans
doing what we were
made perfect in

15. my guardian angel

• 15 •

i wish i could take
u to the world of stars
to make u meet
my guardian angel
-my nanu

16. the day you died

seeing your body gave
chills to my heart
you being
covered in blue sheets
so quite
lying on the ground
all in a hurry
crying in sorrow
screaming at the top of their lungs
i stood there alienated
processing the rush of
world on that 2020's
valentines day
where the real me
came alive

17. therapist

you
yes you dear
you are my personal therapist
the one who saves
me from
breaking

18. grandma's love

her love was sweet like
sugar
her anger was spice like
chilli
she was a walking talking
masterpiece
draped in honey
was her feast
her love for me was like
her own daughter
till date i love her like
my sweet dream

19. being in love

your laugh still
haunts my body
sends chills up
my neck
the touch of your
hands warms my body
your eyes melt my heart
maybe this is what to be
in love feels like

20. a piece of art

she was a piece of art
lean like a tower
smiley like a flower
tall like a tree
eyes day dreamy
truly the most beautiful
girl i had ever seen

21. love

love breaks you
hurts you
twists you
and at the same time scars you

22. GOD

when all the other
doors close
the door to the
eternity opens
the door of the real
faith opens
being of the one and
only mastermind
the ruler of our minds

23. time

i wish i could reverse
the time
freeze it
and be with you again

24. eye contacts

• 24 •

my eyes
crave for your eyes
looking at me
from the other side

25. deadly words

i wish people could
drink their words
and realise
how bitter they
taste

26. favourite person

• 26 •

oh to be someones
favourite person
someones shoulder to
cry and rely on
to be their candle in
darkest night
to be loved by them
the same way you love
them

27. the picture

smile for the picture
dont let the world
see the real you
hide those chaotic
thoughts
this mad world
wont understand them
they will just call you
an idiot

28. voices in your head

• 28 •

even the voices
of your head
get silent
and tired from
the noise and chaos
of this messy world
give them some rest

29. mine

baby can u be
my peace
my night sky
my morning espresso
late evening wine
can u just be
mine

30. shelter

words come to me
rushing like they
need a space to hide

31. poison

i drank the poison
my heart gave me
when my eyes were teary
heart heavy
mind numb
and words frozen
on my tongue

32. being broken

this night is cold
even though it is middle
of the june
i am sipping a hot cup
of tea
writing these poems
after you ended the call
saying it was over
wow dear so easily these three words
burned me and destroyed
me bone to bone
and you didnt even cared

33. home

sometimes you just
need a place or a person
to call your home
your peace
the one who you seek
when your whole
world is falling
apart

34. healing

i know it hurts
but dont worry
you will be okay
time will
heal all your
wounds

35. magician

she creates magic
with her words
that not all can see
or hear

36. unknown fear

• 36 •

i know you are
scared
but what for you
dont know
i dont care even
if this world is against
you i will always
love you

37. secrets

her secrets
could burn down
the world
make all the walls
they laid
fall apart

38. your memories

your memories act
like an old wine
for me
the more that i drink
the more drunk i get

39. seperate ways

i hate the time
we parted our
ways when we could
have stayed together
forever

40. the unaware world

• 40 •

she was a
piece of art
the world was blind

41. fear of being left

• 41 •

i am leaving you
tonight
no longer want those
anxious dreams of
you leaving me

42. be your own love

love like you have never loved
spread kindness like
your wings begging
to soar high
be polite like the clouds
drifting peacefully in the sky
be happy like a child
who just got a brand new toy
in the end
be the one who your heart
seeks to be
but dont be a heartache

43. the escape

• 43 •

the urge to disappear
in a town
where nobody knows you
fall in the ocean
and be a tide
spread your wings and
fly like a bird
just escape this world

44. silent murder

you didnt realised
the way your words
hurted me
and twisted a knife
inside me

45. to be hurt

you screamed at me
beated me
took everything away from
me when
all i needed was love

46. unknown father

every girls first love
is their father
their hero
their ideal type of men
but what about the girls
who never really saw
their father

47. burried love

todays generation

is all about

money

fame

property

love has died under

all these heavy materialistic

words

48. acnes

acnes are a sign of
your beauty
the way they pop
on your skin
breaking all the layers
out of whole strength
but here you are
worrying about
your look

49. ocean

baby i am an ocean
full of storms
dont let yourself
into me
you will drown

50. alcoholic

the person who
would do anything when
they are drunk
create chaos
abuse
hurt you
scream
cry
and then next day
act innocent like
you didnt go
through a zombie acolapse
yesternight with them

50. i miss seeing you

• 51 •

i miss our little
eyecontacts
and then that
smile

51. old love

i adore and admire
the love
our grandparents had
real and worthy
nowadays it is rare to find

52. his sleepy voice

• 53 •

your night voice
takes me to the places
i had never been
oh to be in love

53. stillness of time

i still love you

54. life

• 55 •

life starts with
your loved ones crying
with joy at your birth
and ends with
them crying at your
loss

55. wandering thoughts

• 56 •

my thoughts had
taken me to
places no one
has ever heard of

56. the thoughts of cheater

• 57 •

yes i did mistake
yes i broke
your heart but
cheating on you
broke me too

57. her sunflowers

• 58 •

you are the sunrise
to my sunflowers

58. listener

what broke you
and made you this
how you were before
what makes you happy
what makes you depressed
dont worry dear
i will hear everything from you
and never complaint
because thats
what lovers do

59. i love you

you love old movies
i love you
you love bikes
i love you
you want to travel the whole world
dont worry babe i will
travel with you
you are the darkness
i will be your light
you need a listener
i will be your bride
when you will be in your
eighties
i will still be by your side

60. your notification

the notification
of your messages
sends chills to my body

61. last chance

lets try the last straw
afterall satisfaction is better
than years full of regret

62. what if

what if we make it
turn all our
latenight talks into
reality
what if i be your bride
and you be my
groom

63. to be a mother

• 64 •

being a mother
is the most beautiful
art

64. single parent's child

when you are a
daughter to a
single mother
you had got lots
to achieve to show
this world
that even a single parent can give
birth to a wonderwoman

65. chaos

people who are
born in chaos
love to stay in peace

66. banjara

i am a banjara
searching
for my way
traveling places
like a pligrimage
meeting new people
each day
i am a banjara
searching for my
stay
i had given up all
my materialistic
things to god
i had left all
my loved ones
in sorrow
i just want to be free
free to live in
a hut or a temple
yes i am a banjara
roads are my home
wandering is my way to life

67. starve

loving a writer is hard
you will need to starve
for the words to
come out of their heart

68. 3AM thoughts

i wish to be someones
3 AM thoughts
to bring a smile on their
face when i walk
to be their favourite film
and their darkest secret

69. beautiful boy

i want to be your morning coffee
your afternoon nap
your evening games
and your night time
sleepy voice
i want to be all of you
leave myself and
live in you
oh my darling how are you so beautiful

70. way to heaven

• 71 •

the way your voice
calls my name
takes me to heaven
without even
a single touch

71. make some stories dear

• 72 •

be a little messy
have a little fun
do silly stuff
no matter your age
after all you need to
make some great stories
to recite to your
grandkids

72. the day at the movie
theatre

remember the day at the movie theatre
the way we were sitting next to each other
the lights were off
you were holding my hands
i was blushing hard
i was pretending to see the movie
you were seeing me
the whole time
we kissed eachother alot
i dont remember a single view of
movie only the
way your eyes were staring at me
like i was all you wanted
remember the day at the movie theatre
we almost had our first kiss
and it felt like a dream

73. best friend

the girl
who taught me
the art of living
the fun of dancing
the real meaning of love
who never left me
apart
loved me at my worst
prayed for my success
supported me even if i was
wrong
band aided my wound
and loved me with all
her true heart

74. warrior

she has a whole war going
in her heart and mind
yet she manages to
smile
they say she is dramatic
but no darling
she is a warrior of her
own kind
she is the queen of her
own soul trying
to find the good
in everything but
who explains this to
this cruel world
that she is searching for
her own childhood which she
lost in the war of her
heart and mind
yes she is really a warrior
of her own kind

75. cruelity

why does regret hurts more
than the actual moment,
are we humans only
fond of delivering flowers and
good words at others deaths,
what about when they are alive ?
who injected so much cruelity
in us humans , who is to blame

76. coffee beans

she was like coffee beans
hard from outside,
bitter for few
but once grinded and mixed with the
right person - milk
the best beverage to make
him shimmer
that's why not all people
liked to drink her , they lacked
the patience to make her

77. your eyes

• 78 •

if your eyes were
an ocean
i would drown
in them
whenever you would
cry i would
bring a tsunami in them

78. the day i leave

the day i
leave this world
dont cry
i had been waiting
for this day my
whole life
been a warrior
and a survivor
at the same time
say me off
happily with some flowers
in my hands
say goodbye to my
ashes floating in the sky

79. a young girl

one day i met a
young girl
beautiful like heaven
but scared like hell
her eyes were like flowers
but seemed tired from life
she felt
exhausted from her own flight
her hands were shaking
tears flowing from her eyes
she was hiding all of them
from this messy worlds eyes
all she wanted was peace
she took her coffee and
sat near me
getting burried in a book
even in all those noices
she managed to read half of it
there was silence in her mind
but screams in her heart
maybe we all had met that girl
some of us in that mirror
people passing by

were staring into her soul
but she being lost in her own thoughts
didnt gave them a single glance

80. she

• 82 •

she was quiet like
a heartbreak
and confident like
an actress

81. wish

i wish days come when morning
light makes your heart ignite
when chirping birds
give you a music to dance
on , when you gift
your mother a ring and
she cries with joy ,
when your friends give you a
sweet little surprise
for your birthday ,
when you accomplish your dream,
and get married to the man of
your heart

82. it is going to be ok

i know its been
depressing lately
you are sad
dont know what for
your morning tea tastes
like a bitter toffee
and your heart makes
your days feel a little
heavy
but dont worry love
you got all this
remember leaves too fall before
letting the new ones come
its going to be alright till
then just dance
in the storm

83. mad men

this world will judge you
no matter what you wear
whether you wear a suit
or a saree,
a crop top or a skirt ,
whether you are in a school
uniform or in your
college attire
these mad men wont leave
you they will stare into your
soul and shake the fear in
your bones
maybe they didnt had
mothers or sisters to teach
them how to behave with young girls

84. body shapes

every body shape is sweet
like honey
no matter its pear , apple ,
pineapple or plum
those curves define your
beauty , recite the scenes
of fights you had when you
got ready
dont let this world confuse
you in believing the
fake standard of beauty

85. brown

each and every colour suits
you , makes your whole body
a poetry
the sun lights your skin like
gold, makes it shine like
glitter and
here you are worrying about
your skin colour

86. she not me

one day you will
marry someone
and do all the things
we planned with eachother
you will miss me
when she would be there
playing with your hairs
and not me

87. believe

believe in yourself
young one
dont care a damn about
what others say
behind your back
they are behind you for
a reason

88. be my bet

can u be my bet
even if i defeat
i have nothing to loose
even if i win
i have nothing to win
because you were always mine
i was always yours

89. anger

all that anger rushing
through your blood,
trying to escape from your tongue
no darling dont let those harsh
words escape ,
otherwise what will be the difference left
between you and they

90. deepness

• 92 •

she just wants to sink in the
deepness of her heart
away from
all the chaos
just to understand its
pain..

91. being left

• 93 •

what breaks ur heart
what gives u a heartache
he asked
i replied
being left

92. his care

i love the way you
smile and laugh at the
silly stuff done by your
friends being their partner in crime
your care for them melts me in
disguise

93. his coming

she used to hide her feelings
and stay aloof from the world
until he came to her life and
added magic in it

94. enough of you

if we even talk for
whole 365 days of
the year
still i wont have the
enough of you
and miss you the second
you leave

95. 365 days

i want to spend
each and every 365 day of
my life with
you

96. your heart

i want to become your
heart , breathe in your beats ,
ache when it feels heavy and in
the end die when it stops in you,
with you

97. soul

her soul strived for peace
wanting to scream shutup to all the thoughts,
wanted to stop the war between her
heart and mind,
but she stayed silent
what else could she do
as in the end she was just
her soul

98. dont get tired my love

when your eyes get heavy
and your heart tears apart
dont worry my love
i will give you my everything
to make your world merry again
i will give up my life
to see you smile
and only ask for your love
in return nothing much

99. be with you

i want to be with you
in your highs and lows
ups and downs
tops and bottoms
in your everything my love

100. your presence

i love the way you care for me-
the way no one else has ever done ,
the way no one will ever do ,
your pressence makes my each and
every cell feel special and here
you are asking me if you are
enough

101. blood ,sweat & tears

she knew her first book
wont be a success
but still she wrote it
with all her
blood , sweat and tears

102. her heart & soul

• 104 •

her heart was full of magic
her soul was full of darkness

103. in love

you open me like
an apple
and adore me with a
knife

104. she was different

• •

she had fire in her eyes
and ice in her soul
her heart was glass
and mind of stone

105. hate

who gave right to
others to judge you
remember dear
its always the ones
who cant be you
that hate u
let them hate

106. my man

he was a poem
deep like roots
sweet like flowers
hard to understand
and unknown to most of us
he was a gentlemen by heart
and caring like a father
being carved by god himself
his eyes told stories of his sufferings
his heart was of gold
and body of silver
he truely was a master piece
& deserved an oscar

107. love addicted

love is also a kind
of addiction
the way it keeps
pulling us towards
itself even if we
are hurted , we starve
for the same

108. first kiss

oh how magical was your
first kiss , young boy
do you remember it ,
did it made to your magical
list or was only a lil fling .
tell me young boy
i want to know it all
the way your heart flickered at
that moment
your blood rushed through your skin
as it was your first kiss

109. come with me

after seeing her scars
given to her by her
mother
he pleaded - i promise
my love to take you
away from all this rucous
i promise to never give you
such kind of scar again
trust me &
come with me

110. ego

i want to burn my ego
and inhale its ashes
so that what all i hated
and took personally
could once take me
i want those ashes to go deep
in my lungs and choke
me till death .
yes i want to burn my ego
and inhale its toxic fumes .

111. bridges

i laid my bridges made
of love,
then watched them burn .
and here you are
asking the cause of my scars

112. what i love

when i say i love you
i mean
i love your curly hair in the wind
i love your smiley face
i love the sound of your laugh
i love it when you be dramatic
the way your voice sounds at night
before you sleep
i love all of you from your sweet eyes
to your feet

113. her mother

she was her own creator
and her own destroyer
all the humans came under her
when she was in rage
even the bravest men of the kingdom
feared her
but when she was in love
she was sweeter than the mango
she didnt follow paths
she laid paths
she was the queen of the world
and so the world fell under her

114. dungeon

she had seen her mother suffering ,
she knew who she was ,
she became fearless,
she was ready to start the wars,
the world thought she was just a
young girl
but no dear
she was her own dungeon

115. to lead you home

i hope my writings
touch your heart
and heal the broken
part , sew it close
that was earlier tore
apart .
to spread its magic in
your wings and
take you to your home
that you miss

116. thank you

thank you my dear
for always listening to
me and helping me
survive my messy days

here we come to the end of this unscaled book

my dear reader

i hope you liked reading it and could feel all these

emotions deeply

congratulations you had kept my heart safe in your hands

though this book was not a form of perfection ,

but it itself is my heart and soul

being my first step towards my passion

in the end thankyou for covering this journey

with me

Hope to see you again in my next adventure ...

till then

keep shining

keep spreading love

www.ingramcontent.com/pod-product-compliance
Lightning Source LLC
Chambersburg PA
CBHW031147130726
47988CB00006B/2570